Take Home Skill-Builders
for Spring & Summer

Activities That Involve School, Parents and Child

Written by Ann Richmond Fisher

Illustrated by Ron Wheeler

Teaching & Learning Company

1204 Buchanan St., P.O. Box 10
Carthage, IL 62321-0010

Chiara

This book belongs to

_____

Cover paper sculpture by Gary Hoover

Cover photo by Images and More Photography

ISBN No. 1-57310-119-2

Printing No. 987654321

Teaching & Learning Company
1204 Buchanan St., P.O. Box 10
Carthage, IL 62321-0010

Table of Contents

Dear Teacher or Parent,

Take Home Skill-Builders for Spring & Summer is a wonderful collection of family homework activities for early learners. This book provides the classroom teacher with a fun way to involve the students' families in the learning process. The family "helper" will not be just a silent observer but an active participant in the pages that follow. And we guarantee that the activities are "family friendly"—not too lengthy or difficult to put off parents! Students will have fun practicing important skills with the help of someone very important at home.

This book is also "teacher friendly," containing everything you will need to make this project successful. There is a reproducible letter that will explain the *Take-Home* idea to families, a table of contents to help you locate material quickly and an answer key in the back for selected activities. In addition, each activity is clearly labeled with the featured skill and the seasonal date to which it corresponds.

Activities are arranged chronologically throughout the spring and summer seasons. There are general pages for spring and summer, in addition to pages for specific days such as St. Patrick's Day, Mother's Day and the Fourth of July. Usually the easier pages in each section appear first.

Skills covered include the alphabet, numbers, beginning sounds, spelling, vocabulary, arithmetic, geometry, history, geography, following directions, noting details and many more. For each month of spring and summer you will find several appropriate and important skills for any primary class. You will notice that on some pages the directions seem a bit difficult for young students. That is where the family helper can be called upon. There are also extension activities on many pages that allow the student and helper to "personalize" the exercise, to discuss the topic further or to work a little harder. You may wish to make these optional at times.

Best wishes for an exciting spring and summer as your students, and their families, dive into these *Take Home Skill-Builders for Spring & Summer.*

Sincerely,

Ann

Ann Richmond Fisher

Dear Family,

This spring and summer our class will be working on some *Take Home Skill-Builders for Spring & Summer.* These are short, interesting activities that your child will be asked to complete at home with the help of someone in your family. I hope that you and your child will spend a few enjoyable minutes together completing each one that is sent home.

There will be a wide range of activities including word puzzles coloring pages, math fun and much more. Often there is a related topic for family discussion. The purpose of these assignments is three-fold:

1. to have your child practice the skill featured on each page

2. to teach responsibility of taking the page home, completing it and returning it on time

3. to involve the family in your child's schoolwork

You can help your child by reading the directions together, discussing possible solutions and helping him or her to neatly supply the solutions. Some pages will require more of your help than others. Each page includes a due date and a place for your signature. Occasionally you may need a dictionary, atlas or some other reference book to help you complete a page. If these aids are not available in your home, just do your best.

I trust that you will find many enjoyable activities coming to your home this spring and summer. Please encourage your child to complete each one, if at all possible. Thank you in advance for your support and participation. I value your time and your input, and your child will, too!

Sincerely,

_____
Teacher

March Madness

Cut out the boxes below where the name of this month, March, is written correctly. Then glue them on a piece of paper and draw a picture of something that happens in March.

hcram

March

Marcn

hcram

Monch

Marcn

Macch

March

March

Maɔɔh

Mach

Due: _____

Helper: _____

TLC10119 Copyright © Teaching & Learning Company, Carthage, IL 62321-0010

March

With your family helper, complete this calendar for March of this year. Fill in the name of the month, the year, the missing days of the week and all the dates.

🍀 for St. Patrick's Day   🎂 for any family birthdays

__ __ __ __ __ __					_____ year	
Sunday		Tuesday	Wednesday		Friday	

Find a good place at home to hang the calendar so you can look at it every day.

Before you copy this to give to your students, be sure to write down any school holidays or special events for that month.

Helper: _____

TLC10119 Copyright © Teaching & Learning Company, Carthage, IL 62321-0010

March

General

Due: _____

Like a Lion

An old weather prediction says that if March comes in "like a lion," it will go out "like a lamb." This means that the weather in March can be ferocious like a lion or mild and gentle like a lamb. Complete these expressions where we commonly say one thing is like something else. Use a word you've heard before or think of one of your own. Discuss each expression with your family helper.

Skill

Vocabulary, analogies

as busy as a _____   as happy as a _____

as hungry as a _____   as silly as a _____

as proud as a _____   as cold as _____

as smooth as _____   as flat as a _____

as slippery as a _____   as hard as a _____

March

General

GRUMBLE
GRUMBLE

Due: _____

Helper: _____

Emergency

It is Poison Prevention Month which is a good time to talk with your family helper about how to handle emergencies. Here is the phone number to call for any emergency such as a fire at your house, or if someone has accidentally taken a poison: 911. Learn this number.

Write it here four times. _____,

_____, _____, _____.

Now practice calling this number on a play phone.

Answer these questions about important information you could need in an emergency.

1. What is your own address? _____

   _____

2. What is your own phone number? _____

3. What is a phone number where someone in your family can be

   reached during the day? _____

4. What is your doctor's name? _____

Review this information often with your family.

Helper: _____

Due: _____

Do's and Don'ts

Read each statement with your family helper. Decide if each is a DO or a DON'T and circle the correct word.

Do	Don't	take medicines meant for someone else.
Do	Don't	swallow anything from an unmarked bottle.
Do	Don't	follow the directions on all medicine.
Do	Don't	keep cleaners out of the reach of children.
Do	Don't	take candy from someone you do not know.
Do	Don't	have supervision when you take aspirin, cough syrup, etc.
Do	Don't	smell the fumes from glue, gasoline or other similar products.

Due: _____

Helper: _____

Pig Picture

Here is a pig poking through pea pods. Color the pig and the pea pods because both start with *P*. Then look for other *P* words in the picture and color them, too.

Skill

Beginning sounds

March

National

Pig Day

Helper: _____

Due: _____

Rhyming Riddles

A hairpiece for a hog could be a "pig wig."
Think of a rhyming name for each item below.

Skill

*Vocabulary,
rhyming words*

1. a plump kitten _____ _____

2. a large plant at no cost _____ _____

3. a damp, favorite animal _____ _____

4. a sugary purple vegetable _____ _____

5. the correct evening _____ _____

6. light brown metal container _____ _____

7. a happy father _____ _____

With your family helper, write five new pairs of rhyming words below.

_____   _____

_____   _____

_____   _____

_____   _____

_____   _____

March

National
Pig Day

Due: _____

Helper: _____

Happy Birthday, Dr. Seuss!

Here are the names of some popular books written by Dr. Seuss whose birthday is March 2.

One Fish, Two Fish, Red Fish, Blue Fish

And to Think I Saw It on Mulberry Street

The Grinch Who Stole Christmas

The Cat in the Hat

Green Eggs and Ham

Horton Hears a Who

If possible, read a Dr. Seuss book with your family helper. Pick out one or two of your favorite sentences and copy them here.

_____

_____

_____

_____

Below draw a picture to go with your sentence.

Skill
Reading

March 2
Birthday of
Dr. Seuss

Helper: _____   Due: _____

Skill

Creative writing

The Cat in the Hat is one of the most famous books written by Dr. Seuss. If possible, read it with your family helper to remember all the fun and trouble the cat causes while Mother is away. Then think about what would happen if the cat came to your house. What would you do? What could the cat get into? What fun things could happen? What problems might there be?

Talk about your ideas with your family helper. Then think how your ideas could be written as a story. Finally, tell your story to your family helper who can write it here for you. Draw a picture on the back to go with your new story.

_____
title

_____

_____

_____

_____

_____

_____

March 2

Birthday of
Dr. Seuss

_____

_____

_____

Due: _____

Helper: _____

Phone Book

Since Alexander Graham Bell sent the first phone message back in 1876, millions of people have owned and used telephones. To keep track of all these names and numbers, people use telephone directories, where people's names and numbers are listed in alphabetical order. Put these last names in order by numbering them from 1 to 15.

_____ Smith		_____ Grant	
_____ Miller		_____ Yunker	
_____ Eckhardt		_____ Wilde	
_____ O'Connell		_____ Richmond	
_____ Thompson		_____ Koch	
_____ Pohutski		_____ Armstrong	
_____ Ballard		_____ Haller	
_____ Crabill			

If you have a phone directory, try to find your family's name in it.

Helper: _____

Due: _____

Phone Math

Just in time for the anniversary of the telephone, the Price-Right Phone Company has designed a new way to find the price of phone calls. They simply spell the name of the person being called, and make each letter of the name cost the same in cents as the number on its push button. For example, to find the cost of phoning Amy Lou, add the numbers on each letter's button:

A = 2, M = 6, Y = 9, L = 5, O = 6 and U = 8.

2 + 6 + 9 + 5 + 6 + 8 = 36

So, to phone Amy Lou, the cost would be 36 cents.

Look at the names below. Which name do you think will cost the most? Circle it. Which name do you think will cost the least? Underline it. Now find the actual price of phoning each and write it in the blank.

1. Joy Green　_____

2. Bo Jones　_____

3. Pam Chang　_____

4. Gary Gray　_____

5. Ann Fisher　_____

6. Ed Hunt　_____

7. Kim Lee　_____

Now write the names of two people in your family. Circle the one that you think will cost the most. Then find the prices.

_____

_____

Due: _____

Helper: _____

16

Coded Message

March 10 is the anniversary of the very first telephone message sent in 1876. Alexander Graham Bell sent it to his assistant, Mr. Watson. To find out what that message was, first solve each subtraction problem and write the answer in the first box. Then find that number in the code and write the matching letter in the second box under each problem.

Skill

Subtraction

Code

0 = N	1 = W	2 = C	3 = E	4 = H	5 = M	6 = A
7 = R	8 = O	9 = T	10 = S	11 = U	12 = I	13 = Y

10 - 5	11 - 4

.

8 - 7	12 - 6	18 - 9	15 - 5	13 - 5	9 - 9

,

6 - 4	16 - 8	11 - 6	8 - 5

12 - 8	11 - 8	14 - 7	12 - 9

.

12 - 0

10 - 9	13 - 7	0 - 0	15 - 6

14 - 1	14 - 6	15 - 4

.

March 10

Anniversary of first telephone message

Helper: _____

Due: _____

Irish Dots

Ireland is known as the land where St. Patrick lived long, long ago. It is also known as a country full of beautiful ancient buildings–castles, abbeys, churches and monasteries. Connect the dots in order to see how one of these buildings may have looked hundreds of years ago.

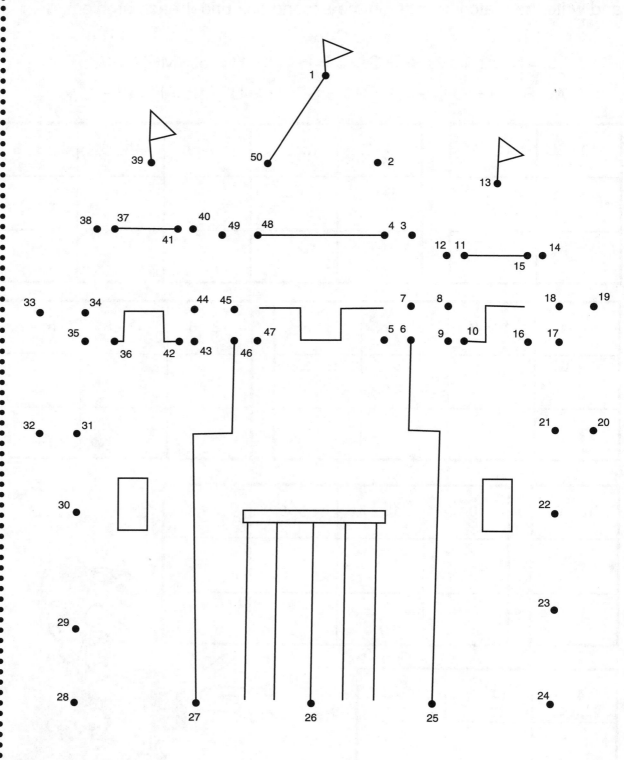

March 17

St. Patrick's Day

Due: _____

Helper: _____

TLC10119 Copyright © Teaching & Learning Company, Carthage, IL 62321-0010

Two in One

This island of Ireland, where St. Patrick lived and worked hundreds of years ago, is now divided into two countries. Here are the flags. Follow the numbers to color them correctly.

1 = green   2 = white   3 = blue

4 = orange   5 = red

Tricolor

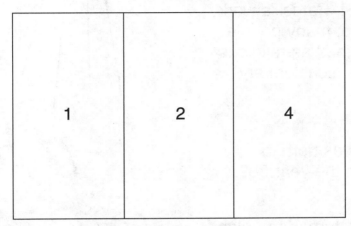

**Republic of Ireland
(Independent country)**

Union Jack

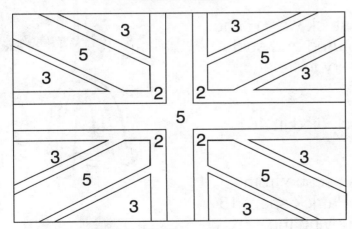

**Northern Ireland
(Part of the United Kingdom)**

With your family helper, find these countries on a world globe or map.

Helper: _____

TLC10119 Copyright © Teaching & Learning Company, Carthage, IL 62321-0010

March 17
St. Patrick's Day

Due: _____

Who Was St. Patrick?

Learn about the man for whom March 17 is named as you put important events of his life in order. Number the statements from 1 to 7 to show which came first, second and so on.

Skill

Sequencing

_____ When Patrick was 22 years old, he escaped his life of slavery and returned to Britain.

_____ During St. Patrick's work in Ireland, many people were trained as religious teachers, scholars and monks.

_____ Patrick was born in Britain in the year 389.

_____ Patrick returned to Ireland to work as a missionary in 432 after his years of study.

_____ When Patrick was 16, he was captured and sold into slavery in Ireland.

_____ St. Patrick died in 461.

_____ After his escape from slavery, Patrick spent 15 years studying the Christian religion.

March 17

St. Patrick's Day

Helper: _____

Speaking of Irish . . .

St. Patrick lived and worked in Ireland over 1500 years ago. Many people in Ireland still read, write and speak the Irish (or Gaelic) language today that was used back in St. Patrick's time. Match each Irish word from the word list with the correct English word by fitting it into the criss-crossed boxes.

GAELIC Dictionary

Note: Only one word will fit properly into each crossword.

**Word List
(and pronunciations)**

cuig (koo ig)

eala (ee la)

haon (hane)

iasc (ee esk)

luch (luck)

madra (ma dra)

teach (chock)

uisce (ish ka)

failte (foil ta)

gruaig (groo ig)

spúnóg (spoon oag)

napáistí (na posh tee)

sneachta (shnock ta)

SNOW

SPOON

HOUSE

CHILDREN

ONE

DOG

WELCOME

HAIR

MOUSE

FIVE

FISH

WATER

SWAN

March 17

St. Patrick's Day

Practice saying these Irish words with your family helper.

Helper: _____

Due: _____

March 17 is the day we honor St. Patrick, the man who brought Christianity to Ireland. Here is a map that shows the island of Ireland. Working with your family helper, follow the directions to correctly label some of Ireland's major cities and the waters that surround it. Write each bold-faced name in the correct blank.

* Capital city

• City

Skill

Map skills

1. **Belfast** is the capital city of Northern Ireland.
2. **Dublin** is the capital of the Republic of Ireland.
3. The city north and west of Belfast is **Londonderry**.
4. The city farthest south is **Cork**.
5. The city east and slightly north of Cork is **Waterford**.
6. The city almost directly west of Dublin is **Galway**.
7. South of Galway and north of Cork is the city of **Limerick**.
8. The **Irish Sea** is east of Ireland.
9. The **Atlantic Ocean** is both west and south of Ireland.
10. **St. George's Channel** is southeast of the island.

March 17

St. Patrick's Day

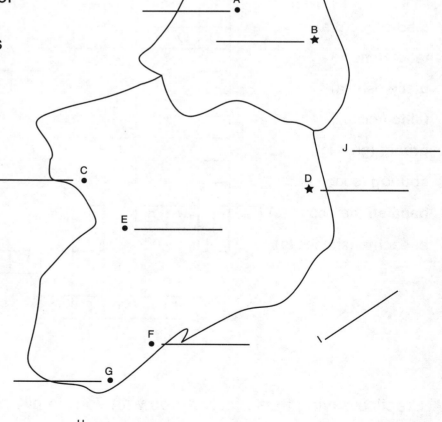

Due: _____

Helper: _____

Tree Time

National Agriculture Day is in March, but many plants grow all year long to give us good food to eat. The description in each box tells how an apple tree changes from season to season. Draw a tree in each box to match the sentence.

Spring: The apple tree is covered with small flowers called blossoms, and it begins to grow tiny green leaves.	**Summer:** The apple tree now has lots of healthy, green leaves and small, growing apples.
Fall: The apples are ripe and ready to pick.	**Winter:** The apple tree loses its leaves and "rests" for the winter.

March 21

National Agriculture Day

Helper: _____

Due: _____

Related Jobs

There are fewer farmers by far today than there were years ago, but they are still able to supply us with plenty of food. Besides farming, there are many other jobs in the United States that are related to farming. For instance, think of the truck driver who hauls canned vegetables from the cannery to the grocery store.

Now brainstorm with your family helper to list as many jobs as possible that are related to agriculture. Think about every step in getting the food planted, grown, harvested, processed, prepared and served. Try to think of 10 or more.

Skill

Creative thinking

1. _____

2. _____

3. _____

4. _____

5. _____

6. _____

7. _____

8. _____

9. _____

10. _____

March 21

National Agriculture Day

Due: _____

Helper: _____

Growing Plans

Five farming friends all grow something different. Use the clues to match each person to the correct product.

Clues

1. Phil raises animals.

2. Rowena does not raise corn.

3. Vania does not raise grain.

4. Dale sells meat and wool.

Draw your farm below.

Farmers	Product
Vania	corn
Caleb	wheat
Rowena	cattle
Phil	sheep
Dale	tomatoes

March 21

National Agriculture Day

Talk with your family helper about a farm you have visited.

Helper: _____   Due: _____

25

Colored Egg

Here is an Easter egg for you to color. Have your family helper read the directions to you as you follow them carefully.

Skill

Left, right, colors

1. Start at the right. Count over to the third stripe. Color it yellow.

2. Start at the left. Count over to the second stripe. Color it purple.

3. Start at the left. Count over to the fourth stripe. Color it orange.

4. Find the first stripe on the right. Color it green.

5. Start at the right. Count over to the fifth stripe. Color it red.

6. Find the first stripe on the left. Color it yellow.

7. Color the remaining stripe blue.

Easter

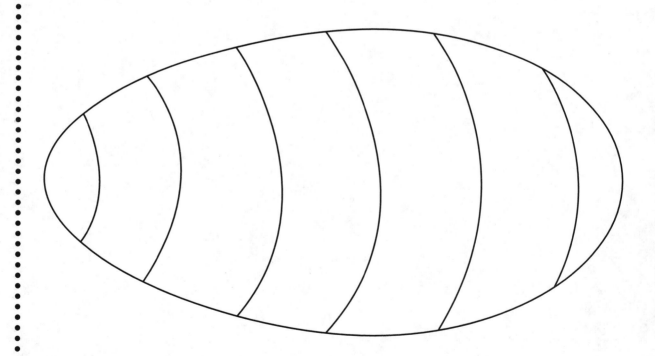

Due: _____

Helper: _____

Easter Treats

The "Eggs"pert Candy Company has asked you to invent a new kind of treat for this Easter. Talk to your family helper about ideas for new types of eggs, bunnies or chocolates.

Give your treat a name: _____

Describe your treat. _____

_____

_____

Draw a picture of your new candy.

Skill
Creative thinking

Easter

Helper: _____

Due: _____

Baby Animals

You may see baby rabbits around Easter time. You probably know that baby rabbits are called bunnies. Do you know the names for other baby animals? Read the words below with your family helper and talk about the correct name for each one's young. Write the answer in the blank.

Skill

Vocabulary

1. cow _____

2. dog _____

3. cat _____

4. goat _____

5. chicken _____

6. bear _____

7. sheep _____

8. deer _____

9. duck _____

10. horse _____

Easter

Due: _____

Helper: _____

Bunnies and Eggs

See how many blanks you can fill in a short amount of time as you "brainstorm" with these questions. If you like, have your family helper write the answers as you think of them.

1. Easter bunnies are very popular. How many words can you think of that rhyme with *bunny*? _____

   _____

2. How many other animals can you list that begin with *B*? _____

   _____

3. Eggs are also very popular at Easter time. How many different ways can you think of to prepare eggs?_____

   _____

4. Easter begins with *EA*. How many other words do you know that begin with *EA*? _____

   _____

5. What are the names of the different parts of an egg? _____

   _____

Easter

6. How many animals can you name that lay eggs? _____

   _____

Helper: _____   Due: _____

TLC10119 Copyright © Teaching & Learning Company, Carthage, IL 62321-0010

29

Fair for Four

Four sisters have just finished an Easter egg hunt. Each one collected an assortment of treats and gifts. The girls decide they all want to have equal numbers of each item. Look carefully at what is in each basket. Then fill in the blanks below.

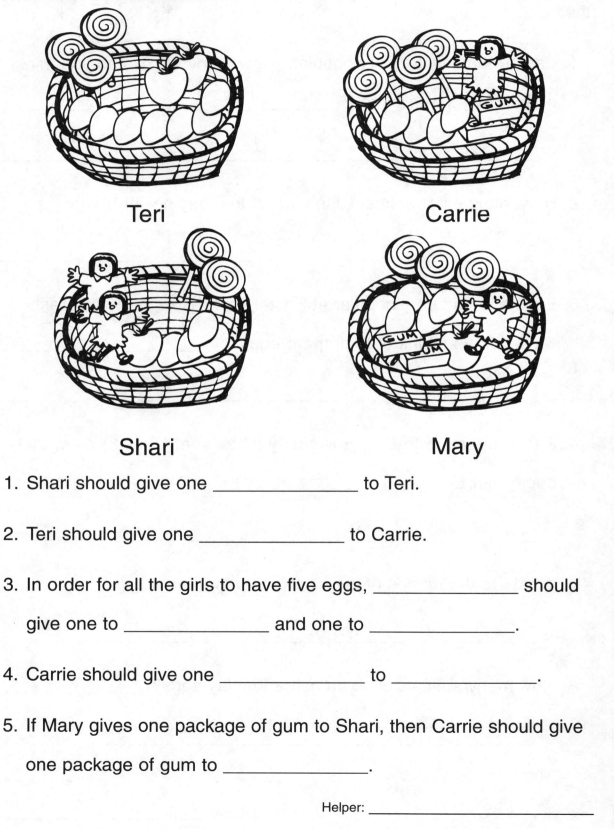

Teri   Carrie

Shari   Mary

1. Shari should give one _____ to Teri.

2. Teri should give one _____ to Carrie.

3. In order for all the girls to have five eggs, _____ should

   give one to _____ and one to _____.

4. Carrie should give one _____ to _____.

5. If Mary gives one package of gum to Shari, then Carrie should give

   one package of gum to _____.

Due: _____

Helper: _____

April Showers

An old expression says, "April showers bring May flowers." In many places, spring does bring a lot of rain which is good for all the new flowers, crops and other plants. With your family helper, keep track of the rainfall during April for your area. By each date below, write an *R* on the blank if it rains that day. If possible, also try to find out how much it rains. Watch a television weather report, look in the newspaper or check your own rain gauge to learn the amount of rainfall each day. Write that in the blank, too. Then have your family helper assist you in finding the total for the month.

Date	Rainfall Amount	Date	Rainfall Amount
1	_____	16	_____
2	_____	17	_____
3	_____	18	_____
4	_____	19	_____
5	_____	20	_____
6	_____	21	_____
7	_____	22	_____
8	_____	23	_____
9	_____	24	_____
10	_____	25	_____
11	_____	26	_____
12	_____	27	_____
13	_____	28	_____
14	_____	29	_____
15	_____	30	_____

Total number of days it rained in April: _____. Total amount of rain: _____.

Helper: _____

Due: _____

Time to Change

In April most of us turn our clocks ahead one hour. Look at each clock below. In the blank under each clock, write what time it will be if the clock is moved ahead one hour.

Then draw the hands on the clocks at the bottom of the page to show what time it will be one hour after the times shown.

_____   _____   _____

_____   _____   _____

April

General

Due: _____   Helper: _____

Animal Antics

National Humor Month is a great time to learn some new jokes. Below are 10 jokes, all about animals. Read through the questions and answers with your family helper to see how they can be paired up to make good jokes. Write the letter for each answer in the correct blank.

_____ 1. What would a gorilla use to fix a car?

_____ 2. Why do dragons sleep during the day?

_____ 3. What is the biggest ant in the world?

_____ 4. Why can't leopards hide very well?

_____ 5. Where does an elephant keep his spare tire?

_____ 6. What is as large as an elephant but weighs nothing?

_____ 7. Where does a skunk sit in church?

_____ 8. What did the boy octopus say to the girl octopus?

_____ 9. Why did the elephant cross the playground?

_____ 10. When is it time to buy a new alarm clock?

A. Because they are always spotted

B. In a pew

C. When an elephant sits on it

D. So they can fight knights

E. I want to hold your hand, hand, hand, hand, hand, hand, hand, hand.

F. A giant

G. To get to the other slide

H. A monkey wrench

I. An elephant's shadow

J. In his trunk

April

National Humor Month

What is your favorite joke? Tell it to your family helper.

Helper: _____

Silly Stories

During National Humor Month, make up a story using one of these titles. Have your family helper assist you with spelling and sentences. Be ready to share your silly story with your class.

How the Cow Jumped over the Moon

The First Pig in Space

The Talking Pumpkin

The Craziest Day of My Life

The Man Who Couldn't Stop Laughing

How the Porcupine Was Named

The Monkey with 10 Tails

How the Elephant Got Its Trunk

_____

_____

_____

_____

_____

_____

_____

_____

_____

April

National
Humor
Month

Due: _____

Helper: _____

Fill in the Blanks

Here is a good way to write a funny story. First think of a word for each numbered description below. Make one list for yourself, and ask your family helper to make a separate list with different words. Then read the story aloud, first adding your numbered words in the matching blanks. Finally, read the story a second time with your helper's list. Enjoy the fun!

1. common noun (thing) _____
2. proper noun (name of a place) _____
3. proper noun (name of another place) _____
4. verb (action word) in the past _____
5. another verb in the past _____
6. another verb in the past _____
7. common noun (place) _____
8. common noun (person) _____
9. adjective (describing word) _____
10. adjective (another describing word) _____
11. noun (place) _____

Story

Last week I lost my __1__. I traveled from __2__ to __3__ looking for it. I didn't know what to do. I __4__, and I __5__, and I __6__. Finally, I found my __1__. It was under my __7__! I was so excited that I showed it to my __8__. The only thing different about it was that it was now __9__ and __10__. I guess I learned my lesson. To keep my __1__ safe, next time I will keep it in a __11__.

April

National Humor Month

Helper: _____

Due: _____

Number Lines

Math Education Month is a good time to check how well you know your numbers. First find the number 1. Then draw a line from 1 to 2 to 3 and so on until you reach 20. Beware! There are some backwards numbers that you won't use.

Skill

Counting to 20

7 18 10
13 2 ⌐
12 16
17 4
3 8 5
19 20 9
14 11
1
Ɛ̵ 15 6

April

Math
Education
Month

Try to count to 50 or 100 for your family helper.

Due: _____

Helper: _____

36

Hidden Numbers

Here is a special bit of fun for Math Education Month. Can you find seven number words hidden in the paragraph below? Underline the number words. As an example, the *eight* could be hidden inside one word: h**eight** or between two words: Let's ride in the sl**eigh t**onight.

Where has the fat worm gone? He was wriggling away from my reel even before I had the hook on it! If I've lost him, I'll be sorry. This evening I came prepared with reel, line and bait hoping to catch plenty of fish. It's not often that a worm of ours gets away!

Practice writing your numbers below.

_____

_____

_____

_____

_____

_____

_____

April

Math
Education
Month

Helper: _____

Due: _____

Measure It!

Math Education Month is a great time to practice the important skills of estimating and measuring. Work with your family helper to first estimate and then measure the lengths of these items around your house.

Inches	**Estimate**	**Measurement**
1. the height of a drinking glass	_____	_____
2. the height of a lamp	_____	_____
3. your own height	_____	_____
4. your family helper's height	_____	_____
5. the width of a table	_____	_____

Feet		
6. the length of your bed	_____	_____
7. the height of a doorway	_____	_____
8. the length of your foot	_____	_____

Yards		
9. the length of your living room	_____	_____
10. the length of the outside of your home	_____	_____

April

Math
Education
Month

Due: _____

Helper: _____

Picture Pairs

Pictured below are things that can be recycled. Below the items are pictures of what these things might look like from the top. Draw lines to connect the pictures that match.

Helper: _____

Trash Cash

Imagine on Earth Day that you could go to a recycling center and turn your trash into cash. Here is how you could decide what your garbage is worth.

- Look at the letters in the name of the trash.
- Count two cents for every vowel.
- Add five cents for every consonant.

For example, *tin can* has two vowels (2 x 2) and four consonants (4 x 5), so the total value of a tin can is 4¢ + 20¢ or 24 cents.

Now find out how much these other kinds of trash are worth.

1. soup can _____

2. shoe _____

3. old hat _____

4. flat tire _____

5. magazine _____

6. egg carton _____

7. coffee grounds _____

8. apple core _____

9. glass jar _____

10. plastic bag _____

Due: _____

Helper: _____

Water, Water, Everywhere!

Water is one of Earth's most valuable resources. About three-fourths of the Earth's surface is covered with water in oceans, seas, lakes, ponds and rivers. Think about how you use water every day. With your family helper, list a lot of different things your family uses water for every day.

_____ _____

_____ _____

_____ _____

_____ _____

_____ _____

If you had no water for two days, what would you miss the most? _____

_____

Why? _____

_____

April

Earth Day

Helper: _____   Due: _____

Triangle Trouble

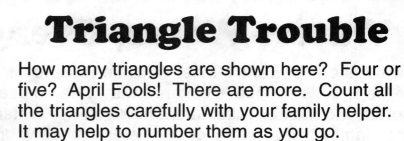

How many triangles are shown here? Four or five? April Fools! There are more. Count all the triangles carefully with your family helper. It may help to number them as you go.

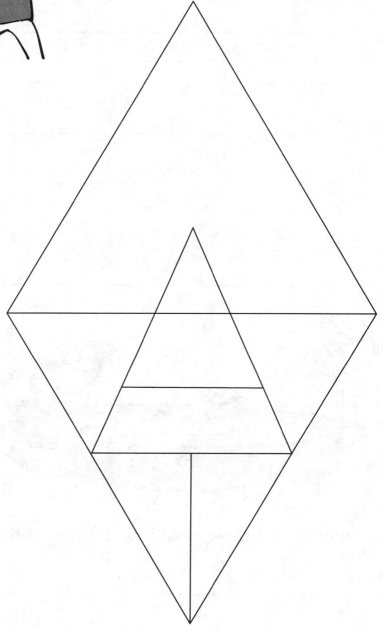

How many did you find? _____

Draw a similar shape with lots of squares. See if you and your family helper can agree on the number of squares inside.

Due: _____

Helper: _____

April

Here is a calendar for April, but it is full of mistakes. Put an *X* on each one that you and your family helper find.

Aqril _____
year

sonday	Monday	Tuesday	Wednesday	Friday	Thursday	Saturday
1	2	3	4	5	6	
8	9	10	11	11	13	14
15	16	17	18	19	20	21
21	23	24	52	26	27	28
29						

April
General

Now work with your family helper to make a correct calendar for April of this year.

Find a good place at home to hang the calendar so you can look at it every day.

Helper: _____ Due: _____

43

Boston Marathon

This map of the United States shows Boston, Massachusetts, home of the famous marathon which began over 100 years ago this month. Answer the questions below with your family helper.

1. Find the state of Michigan and shade it in. If someone were traveling from Michigan to Boston to watch the marathon, in what direction would they travel? _____

2. Find the state of New Hampshire and shade it in. What direction is it from New Hampshire to Boston? _____

3. Find the state of Texas and shade it in. What direction is it from Boston to Texas? _____

4. Find your state on the map and shade it in. In what direction would you have to travel to attend the Boston Marathon? _____

April 19

Anniversary of first Boston Marathon

Due: _____

Helper: _____

Date Data

One of the best-known races in the world is the Boston Marathon. Do you know in what year the first Boston Marathon was held? Use these clues to find the year.

1. For the first digit, use the lowest odd number.

2. For the third digit, use the largest odd number that is less than 10.

3. The second digit is the difference between the third and first digits.

4. The fourth digit is the difference between the second and first digits.

___ ___ ___ ___

April 19

Anniversary of first Boston Marathon

Helper: _____

Due: _____

May Flowers

April showers bring May flowers! Write the letter next to the group it describes. Notice you will have one extra letter.

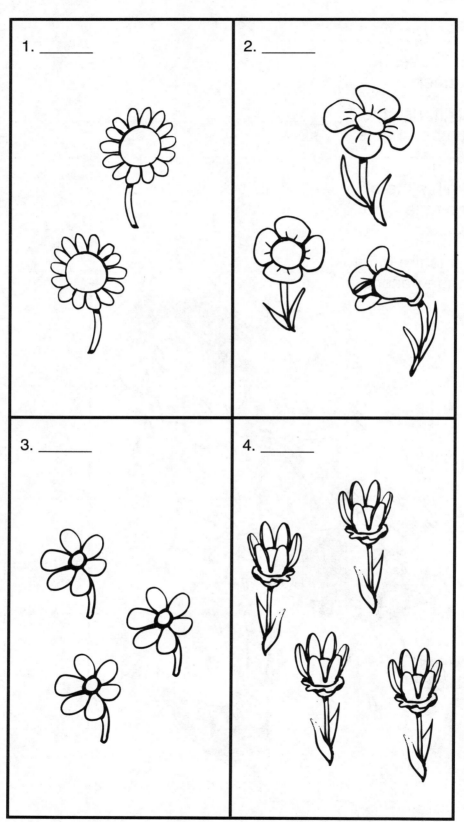

A. Flowers with more than six petals.

B. Flowers with leaves and three or four petals.

C. Flowers with no leaves.

D. Flowers with five or six petals.

E. Flowers with more than four petals but less than six petals and no leaves.

May

General

Due: _____

Helper: _____

May

With your family helper, complete this calendar for May of this year. Fill in the name of the month, the missing year, the missing days of the week and all the dates. Add the names of any family members who are having special days this month.

___	___			___	___	___
Sun.	Mon.		Wed.			Sat.

Now hang your completed calendar in a place where you can see it every day.

Before your copy this to give to your students, be sure to write down any school holidays and special events for that month.

Helper: _____   Due: _____

Family Fitness

With your family helper, list several activities your family likes to do together that also help keep you fit. A few ideas are listed to help you get started.

1. going for a walk

2. swimming

3. playing softball

4. _____

5. _____

6. _____

7. _____

8. _____

9. _____

10. _____

11. _____

12. _____

13. _____

14. _____

15. _____

May

National Physical Fitness and Sports Month

Circle your favorite family activity on the list.

Now plan a time in the next week or two when your family can do one of the activities on your list.

Due: _____

Helper: _____

Criss-Crossed Sports

Read each clue below. Write the name of the sport for which each piece of sports equipment is used in the correct place in the crossword.

Across

3. soccer ball and goal
4. football helmet
6. swimsuit and goggles
7. basketball and hoop
9. hockey stick and puck
10. volleyball and net

Down

1. tennis racquet
2. baseball bat
3. skis and poles
5. bowling ball and pins
8. arrow and target

Skill

Vocabulary

May

National
Physical
Fitness and
Sports Month

Helper: _____

Due: _____

Hoop Shoot

In basketball, when a player makes a field goal (FG) inside the three-point line, that team receives two points. For each free throw (FT), the team receives one point. Find the total number of points each player earned, and then find the total number of points scored for the whole

Skill

Addition

Player's Name	FG	FT	Total
A. Anderson	5	3	_____
B. Basket	2	4	_____
C. Court	6	1	_____
D. Dribble	7	0	_____
E. Ease	3	5	_____
F. Friendly	2	1	_____
G. Goal	4	2	_____
H. Hooper	1	6	_____

Team Total _____

May

National
Physical
Fitness and
Sports Month

Due: _____

Helper: _____

Family Photos

Here are pictures of some of the people in Cathy's family. Follow the directions as your family helper reads them to you.

1. Aunt Esther is wearing a hat. Color it yellow.

2. Find Mom and color her dress red.

3. Cathy's brother, Ron, is wearing a striped shirt. Circle his picture.

4. Cousin Lee wears glasses. Color his shirt brown.

5. Uncle Russ has a beard. Underline his picture.

6. Cathy's grandfather is always smiling. Color his shirt green.

Look at some of your favorite family photos with your family helper.

Helper: _____

Due: _____

Family Time

BREAK!

Talk with your family helper about the things you enjoy doing with your family. Discuss which ones you like best and list three of them here.

1. _____

2. _____

3. _____

Now draw a picture of you and your family doing one of the things on your list.

Helper: _____

Family Tree

This diagram shows part of the Smith family. Jan and Jim married and had four children who are shown underneath them. Two of their children have married. Tom married Cathy and they have three daughters. Bill married Dee and they have two sons.

Use the information from the diagram as you and your family helper answer the questions.

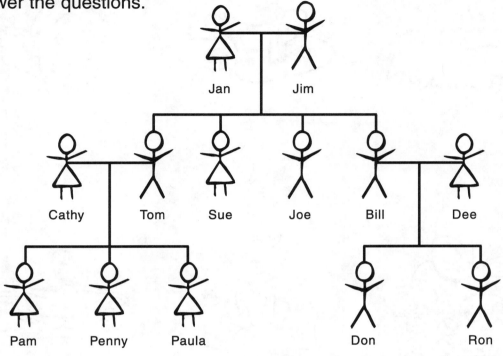

1. How many grandchildren do Jan and Jim have? _____

2. How many brothers does Joe have? _____

3. How many sisters does Sue have? _____

4. Tom has three daughters. How many nephews does he have?

   _____

5. How many uncles does Don have? _____ Who are they?

   _____

6. How many nieces does Sue have? _____

7. How many sisters does Penny have? _____

8. How many cousins does Ron have? _____

9. How many cousins does Pam have? _____

Draw a family tree of part of your family on the back of this sheet.

Helper: _____

Due: _____

In or On?

Each of these animals is waiting for someone special to be kind to them this week. The animals are either *in* or *on* one of their favorite places. Look at each picture and complete the word underneath.

Skill

In and on

1.

___ n

2.

___ n

3.

___ n

4.

___ n

5.

___ n

6.

___ n

First Week in May

Be Kind to Animals Week

7.

___ n

8.

___ n

9.

___ n

Now color the pictures.

Due: _____

Helper: _____

A to Z Animals

Can you think of an animal that begins with each letter of the alphabet? Have someone in your family help you write each animal name in the correct blank below. (Some letters may not be possible.)

Skill
Beginning sounds

A _____   N _____

B _____   O _____

C _____   P _____

D _____   Q _____

E _____   R _____

F _____   S _____

G _____   T _____

H _____   U _____

I _____   V _____

J _____   W _____

First Week in May

Be Kind to Animals Week

K _____   X _____

L _____   Y _____

M _____   Z _____

Helper: _____   Due: _____

Time for Pets

It takes a lot of time to take good care of pets. Here are several things that Carlos will be doing today to take care of his pet dog, Skippy. Number them from 1 to 8 to show what Carlos will be doing first, second and so on.

Skill

Sequencing

_____ 2:00 p.m. Take Skippy to the vet for his shots.

_____ 10:00 a.m. Take Skippy out for exercise. Walk to the park and play fetch.

_____ 8:00 p.m. Be sure Skippy has plenty of fresh water before you go to bed. Let him outside one last time for the night.

_____ 7:00 a.m. Let Skippy outside before breakfast.

_____ 5:00 p.m. Take Skippy out for a long walk.

_____ 8:00 a.m. Give Skippy fresh food and water.

_____ 6:00 p.m. Feed Skippy again.

_____ 3:00 p.m. Clean up any messes Skippy has made in the lawn or on the sidewalk. Make sure his bed is clean and comfortable.

First Week in May

Be Kind to Animals Week

Talk with your family helper about what your pet needs and how you can help.

Due: _____

Helper: _____

Give Me Five!

Cinco de Mayo is a Mexican holiday celebrated on the *fifth* day of the *fifth* month. Search the boxes below for sets that show five. Circle each box that shows five objects or the number 5 drawn correctly. Then color the pictures.

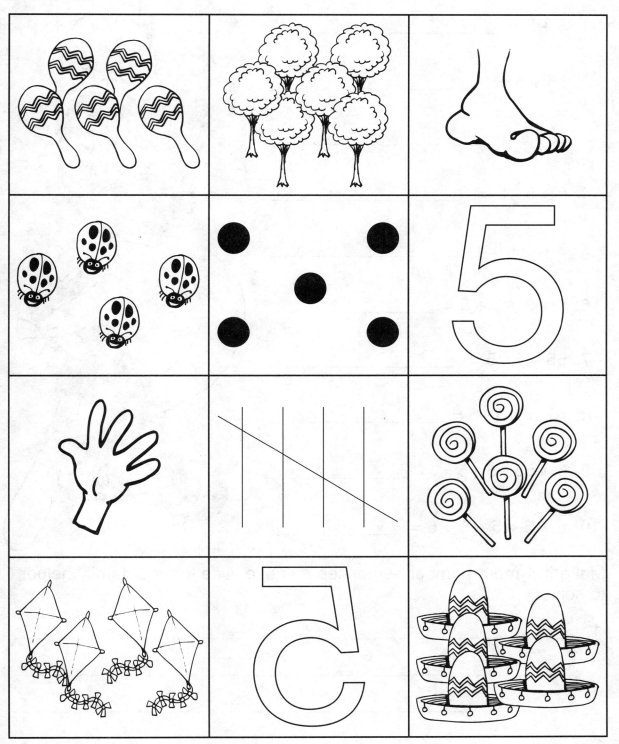

May 5

Cinco de Mayo

With your family helper, look for sets of five in your house.

Helper: _____

Due: _____

Five Facts

Cinco de Mayo is a holiday celebrated on the *fifth* day of the *fifth* month. Here are some number sentences using only *fives*. Write the answer to each one.

1. 5 + 5 = _____

2. 55 + 5 = _____

3. 55 - 5 = _____

4. 5 + 5 - 5 = _____

5. 5 + 5 + 5 = _____

6. 5 + 5 + 5 + 5 = _____

7. 55 + 5 - 5 = _____

8. 5 - 5 + 5 - 5 = _____

9. 5 + 55 - 5 - 5 = _____

10. 5 + 5 + 5 + 5 + 5 = _____

Make five more number sentences that use fives for your family helper to solve.

1. _____

2. _____

3. _____

4. _____

5. _____

Due: _____

Helper: _____

Mexican Mosaic

Celebrate Cinco de Mayo with your family helper by completing this Mexican mosaic. Here's how . . .

- Collect small scraps of colored paper. Try to find a lot of different, bright colors.

- Cut or tear these into small squares, about this size:

- Arrange the squares to make a pattern you like on this piece of pottery.

- Glue the squares in place.

- Cut out your decorated pottery and mount on another piece of paper or cardboard.

Skill

Small motor coordination, creating a pattern

May 5

Cinco de Mayo

Helper: _____

Due: _____

Sweet Treats

A box of chocolates makes a yummy Mother's Day gift. Look at the six boxes of candy below while your family helper reads these directions to you. Then carefully follow each step.

1. Find the boxes that contain the same number of round and square candy pieces. Draw a ring around these boxes.

2. Put an *X* on the box that has the most triangle-shaped pieces.

3. Find the box with the lowest number of squares. Draw a line under it.

4. Find the box with the same number of rectangle and triangle-shaped pieces. Put a ✓ next to this box.

5. Color all the candies in the box that contains no triangles.

6. Draw a line to connect the boxes that hold the same number of pieces.

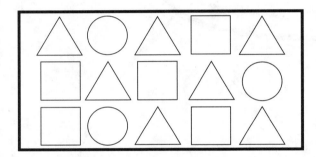
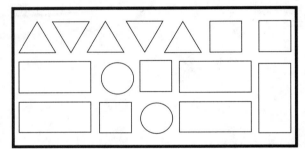

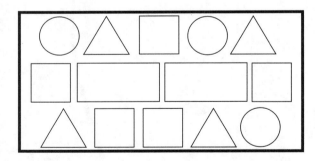
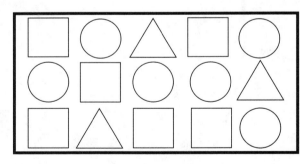

Second Sunday in May

Mother's Day

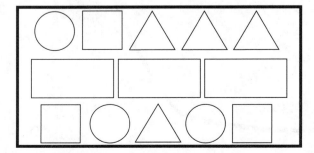
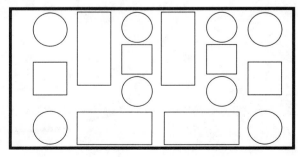

Due: _____

Helper: _____

Mother's Day Dinner

What would you like to serve your mother for a special meal on her special day? With your family helper, plan a meal that your mom would enjoy. List a food for each blank below. Try to pick a variety of healthy foods.

Main course: _____

Vegetable(s): _____

Fruit: _____

Bread or pasta: _____

Dairy product(s): _____

Other foods: _____

_____

_____

_____

_____

_____

Skill

Nutrition, creative thinking

Second Sunday in May

Mother's Day

If possible, choose one item on your list and work with someone in your family to actually prepare it for your mother.

Helper: _____   Due: _____

Fancy or Free?

Think about the special gifts you would like to give your mother this year. First of all, imagine that you had all the money you needed to buy one very fancy, expensive gift. Write a few sentences describing what you would choose and why you think your mother would like it. (Someone in your family can help you with the writing.)

_____

_____

_____

_____

_____

Now think of all the important things you can give your mother that don't cost anything. Your love, a smile and help around the house are a few ideas. Now write a few sentences describing what "free" gifts you can give your mom this year and why you think she would enjoy them.

Second Sunday in May

Mother's Day

_____

_____

_____

_____

Due: _____

Helper: _____

62

Blast Off!

May 26 marks the birthday of Sally Ride, America's first woman in space. Connect these dots to complete a picture about space travel. You will need to count up by fives.

Skill

Counting by fives

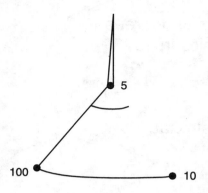

USA

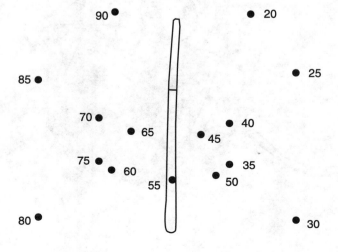

May 26

Birthday of Sally Ride

Helper: _____

Due: _____

Ages and Stages

Sally Ride, America's first woman in space, was born in 1951. Use subtraction to find out how old she was when each event below took place.

1. Sally earned university degrees in English and physics in 1973.

   Age: _____

Work Space

2. Sally became an astronaut candidate in 1978.

   Age: _____

3. In 1983 Sally flew in the *Challenger* space shuttle.

   Age: _____

4. In 1987 she published a report on America's future in space travel and retired from the space program.

   Age: _____

5. Find Sally's age this year.

   Age: _____

May 26

Birthday of Sally Ride

Due: _____

Helper: _____

Memorial Mayhem

Read this story to learn about Memorial Day. You and your family helper will need to unscramble several words in order for it to make sense. Write each word correctly on the blank provided.

Memorial Day is a United **t a t e S s** _____ holiday which honors

all the men and **o n w e m** _____ who have died while serving

their **t c y o r u n** _____. It was first held over 100 **r e y a s**

_____ ago, in 1868, to remember the **o l p e p e** _____

who died in the Civil War. At first, the holiday was on **M y a**

_____ 30. But in most states, Memorial Day is now held on the

last **n a M o d y** _____ in May.

On Memorial Day, many people **s i v t i** _____ the graves of

people who died in wars and place **w l o e s f r** _____ on them.

Many towns hold **r a p d a s e** _____ with marching bands, fire

c r u t s k _____ and more. Some towns have special cere-

monies in a city **r a p k** _____ or cemetery. Because it is a day

off work, many families have **i c n c i p s** _____ or other special

activities. A famous car **c e a r** _____, the Indianapolis 500, is

held on **e o r M i l a m** _____ Day.

Helper: _____

TLC10119 Copyright © Teaching & Learning Company, Carthage, IL 62321-0010

Skill

Context, spelling

Last Monday in May

Memorial Day

Due: _____

65

Spot the Butterflies

Butterflies are a sure sign of spring. In each set, color the butterfly with the most spots. Then find two butterflies on the page that are exactly alike and circle them. Finally, color all the butterflies.

Spring

Due: _____

Helper: _____

Kite Sight

Breezy spring days are the perfect times to fly a kite. Look at the fancy kites here. Finish drawing each one so that both sides match.

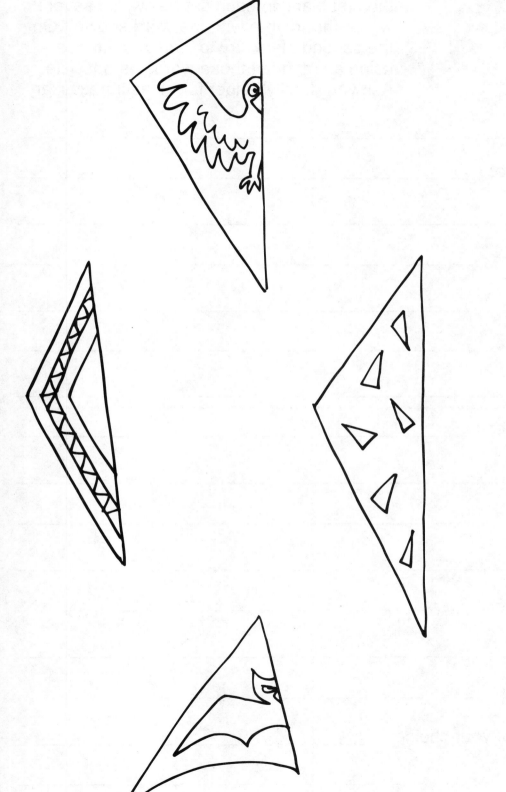

Skill

Symmetry

Spring

Helper: _____

Kite Flight

What a *sight* to see a *bright kite* take its *flight*! Now it's your turn to write fun sentences with rhyming springtime words. On the first blank in each set below, list several words that rhyme with the word shown. On the second blank, try to write a sentence using as many of those words as possible. Ask your family helper for ideas if necessary.

1. spring _____

   Sentence: _____

2. grow _____

   Sentence: _____

3. seed _____

   Sentence: _____

4. green _____

   Sentence: _____

5. sun _____

   Sentence: _____

6. ball _____

   Sentence: _____

7. bloom _____

   Sentence: _____

8. a word of your choice: _____

   Sentence: _____

Spring

Due: _____

Helper: _____

Bargain Hunting

Five friends, Ron, Kim, Jed, Bruce and Darnell, each have brought some coins with them to their neighborhood's first garage sale of the spring. Count the coins in each pile and write their total value in the blank underneath. Then draw a line from each pile to one item each friend can buy with his coins. (Make sure everyone gets to buy something.) Color the items.

Skill

Adding coin values

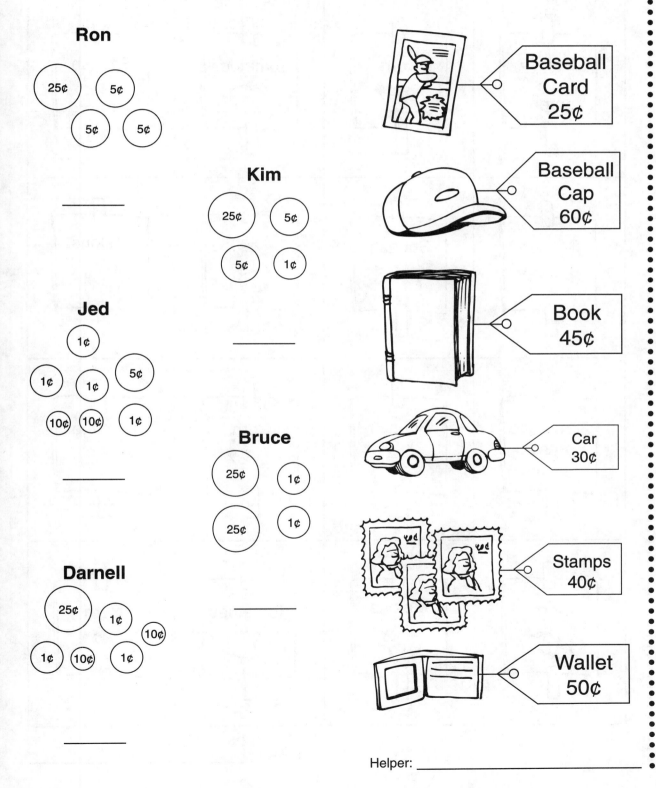

Ron

25¢ 5¢
5¢ 5¢

_____

Kim

25¢ 5¢
5¢ 1¢

_____

Jed

1¢
1¢ 1¢ 5¢
10¢ 10¢ 1¢

_____

Bruce

25¢ 1¢
25¢ 1¢

_____

Darnell

25¢ 1¢
10¢
1¢ 10¢ 1¢

_____

Baseball Card 25¢

Baseball Cap 60¢

Book 45¢

Car 30¢

Stamps 40¢

Wallet 50¢

Spring

Helper: _____

Due: _____

Plan a Plot

Four neighbors are sharing this garden. Flo, Jo, Beau and Moe need to divide this garden so that each has one plot of corn, melons, tomatoes and squash. Each one's share needs to be connected in one piece. Can you and your family helper find a way to divide this garden? Draw in heavy lines to show your answer.

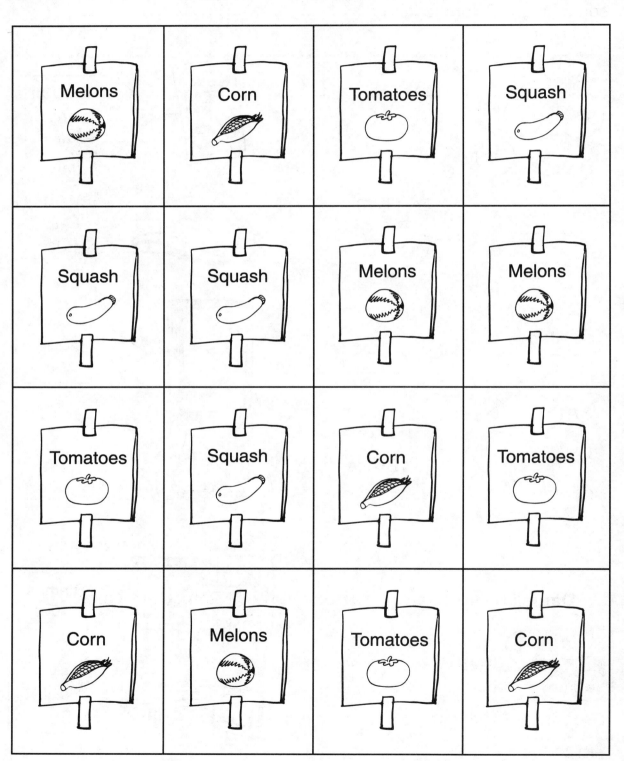

Spring

Due: _____

Helper: _____

Score It

Two baseball teams, the Badgers and the Coyotes, just played their first game of the spring. Use the clues to learn which team won. Write the number of runs scored in each inning on the scoreboard.

Inning	1	2	3	4	5	6	7	8	9	Total
Badgers										
Coyotes										

A. Both teams scored two runs in the first inning.

B. In the second inning, the Badgers scored one run, but the Coyotes didn't score any.

C. In the third and eighth innings, the Coyotes scored two runs and the Badgers scored zero.

D. No runs were scored in the fourth, seventh and ninth innings.

E. The fifth inning was just like the second inning.

F. In the sixth inning, each team scored one more run than they did in the fifth inning.

G. Write the final scores on the scoreboard under *Total*.

Which team won? _____

Helper: _____

Due: _____

Complete the Calendar

With your family helper, make a new calendar for each month this summer. Fill in the name of the month, the missing year, the missing days of the week and all the dates. Add special symbols of your choice for family birthdays and holidays.

					year	
	Monday		Wednesday		Friday	

June, July or August

General

Find a good place at home to hang the calendar so you can look at it every day.

Before you copy this to give to your students, be sure to write down any school holidays or special events for that month.

Due: _____

Helper: _____

Dairy Delights

June is Dairy Month, a good time to appreciate all the good foods that come from milk. Talk with your family helper about dairy foods. Then circle the ones that you find below.

Some dairy products are made from cow's milk. Draw a picture of a cow on the back of this sheet.

Helper: _____

Due: _____

Compound Cones

Match each scoop of ice cream to a cone to spell the name of an ice cream flavor. Draw lines to connect the right parts. Color the scoops and cones.

Skill

Compound words

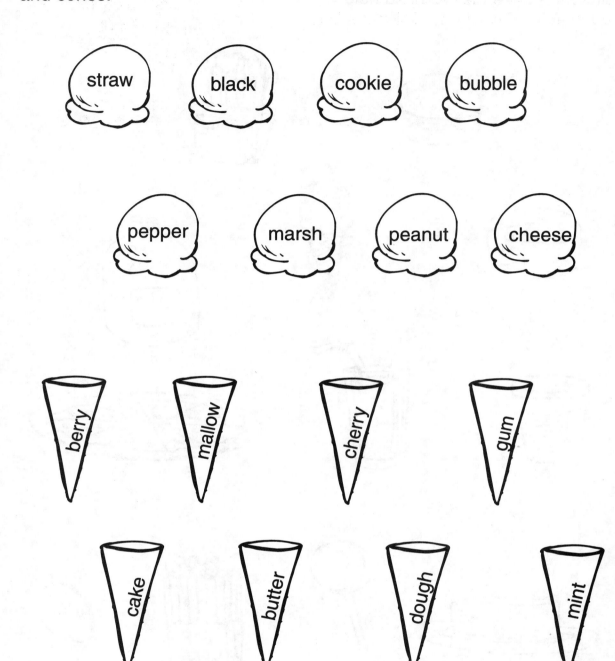

June

Dairy Month

Pick one scoop and match it with a wrong cone. Talk with your family helper about how this new flavor might look and how it might taste.

Due: _____

Helper: _____

Finish the Flag

June 14 is Flag Day in the United States. Count by twos to complete the American flag below. You will connect 50 dots in all—one for each star on the flag! Color the flag.

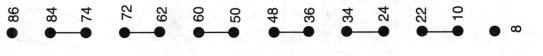

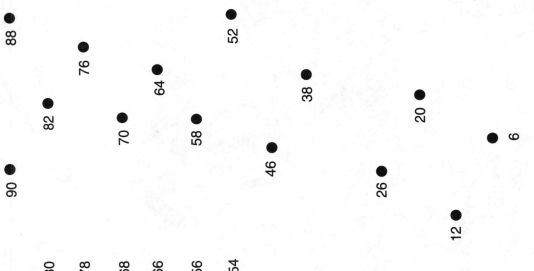

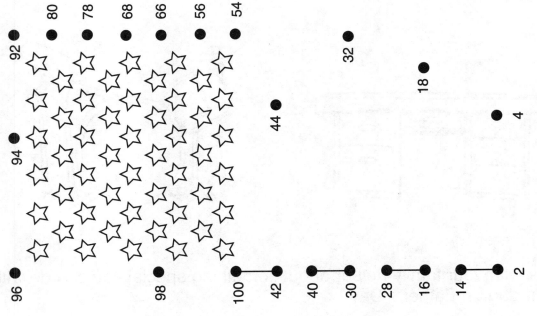

86 · 84 — 74 · 72 — 62 · 60 — 50 · 48 — 36 · 34 — 24 · 22 — 10 · 8

88 · 76 · 64 · 52

82 · 70 · 58 · 38 · 20 · 6

90 · 46 · 26 · 12

92 · 80 · 78 · 68 · 66 · 56 · 54 · 32 · 18 · 4

94 · 44

96 · 98 · 100 — 42 · 40 — 30 · 28 — 16 · 14 — 2

June 14

Flag Day

Helper: _____

Due: _____

TLC10119 Copyright © Teaching & Learning Company, Carthage, IL 62321-0010

Dad's Diversions

Did your **d**ad **d**o something **d**elightful for his **d**ynamic **d**ay? Look at the pictures below of things some dads might use or have fun with on Father's Day. Color the ones that begin with *D*.

Skill

Beginning sounds

Third Sunday in June

Father's Day

Talk with your family helper about something special you can do with your dad on Father's Day.

Due: _____

Helper: _____

Fatherly Facts

Twelve children were asked what they were going to give their dad for Father's Day. Their answers are shown on this graph.

Carefully read each statement below. Use the graph to tell whether or not each sentence is true. Write *true* or *false* in each blank.

_____ 1. More children gave cards than books.

_____ 2. Only two children gave their fathers something to eat.

_____ 3. More children chose neckties than socks.

_____ 4. Equal numbers of children chose books and neckties.

_____ 5. More kids chose books or chocolates than socks.

_____ 6. Half of the children gave their dads something to wear.

_____ 7. An equal number of children chose chocolates and cards.

_____ 8. The number of children who chose socks and cards is the same as the number of children who chose books, chocolates and neckties.

Now write two sentences for your family helper to solve.

_____ 9. _____

_____ 10. _____

Third Sunday in June

Father's Day

Helper: _____   Due: _____

Same Sounds

July is National Picnic Month, so it's time to invite all your relatives to an outdoor meal. Hopefully, **Aunt** Alice won't find an **ant** in her food! Notice the words *aunt* and *ant* sound alike but have different meanings and spellings. They are called homonyms.

For each word below, think of a homonym. Then try to write a sentence about your picnic that uses both words.

meat _____

Sentence: _____

pear _____

Sentence: _____

ate _____

Sentence: _____

bee _____

Sentence: _____

blew _____

Sentence: _____

July

National
Picnic Month

Due: _____

Helper: _____

Sit Fit

Seven people will be seated at this picnic table. Use the clues to find out where each person should sit. Write each name in the correct place.

1. Emily wants to sit on the end.

2. Randy will sit on Emily's left.

3. Josh will sit between Vic and Kim.

4. Vic wants to sit next to Emily.

5. Irv will sit across from Kim.

6. Susan will sit next to Irv.

July

National Picnic Month

Helper: _____

Due: _____

Happy Birthday, USA!

July 4, 1776, was the day the United States of America officially adopted the Declaration of Independence, and so the day is known as the birthday of the country. The USA is now over 220 years old, but July 4 is still a day to celebrate! Use your pencil, crayons or markers to decorate this huge birthday cake for America's birthday this year.

Skill

Creative thinking

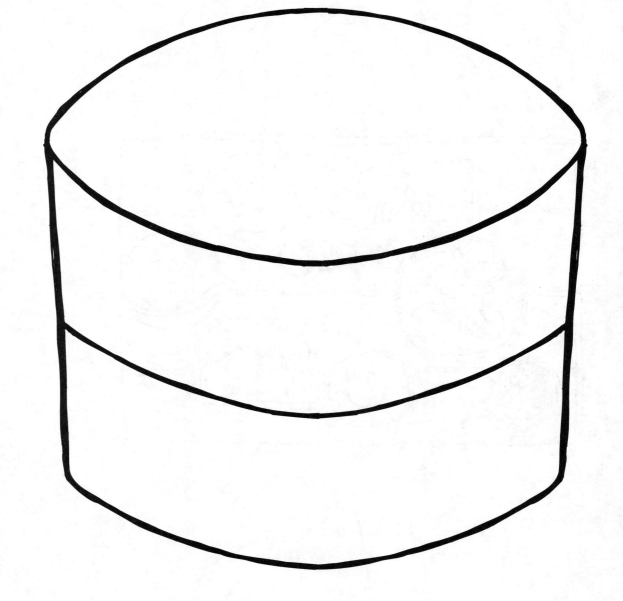

July 4

Independence Day

Due: _____

Helper: _____

The Fourth Challenge

For the Fourth of July, can you find at least 15 words spelled only with the letters in *Fourth of July*? Work with your family helper to list your words here.

Three-Letter Words	Four-Letter Words	Longer Words
hot	roof	froth
_____	_____	_____
_____	_____	_____
_____	_____	_____
_____	_____	_____
_____	_____	_____
_____	_____	_____
_____	_____	_____
_____	_____	_____
_____	_____	_____
_____	_____	_____
_____	_____	_____
_____	_____	_____
_____	_____	_____
_____	_____	_____

July 4
Independence Day

Helper: _____

Due: _____

One Small Step

On July 20, 1969, U.S. astronaut Neil Armstrong became the first man to walk on the moon. His first words have become very famous: "That's one small step for man, one giant leap for mankind."

Skill

Creative writing

Imagine what it would have been like if *you* were the first person to step on the moon. How would you have felt–excited, frightened, proud? What would you have seen? Talk about your ideas with your family helper. Then together write a letter to your family back home on Earth telling them what it was like to walk on the moon.

Dear Family,

_____

_____

_____

_____

_____

Now suppose an alien becomes the first from his planet to step on Earth, and imagine that he starts in *your* backyard. What would he see? How would he feel? What would he say? Talk about your ideas with your family helper. Then write a brief note that the alien might send to his family.

Dear Family,

_____

_____

_____

_____

_____

July 20

Anniversary of first moon landing

Due: _____

Helper: _____

Calendar Quiz

See if you and your family helper can find answers to these questions about the month of August. For some of the questions, you will need to look at a calendar for August of this year.

1. How many days are in the month of August? _____

2. What other months of the year have the same number of days?

_____

3. If August 1 is on a Monday, then what day of the week will these dates be:

    August 2 _____   August 3 _____

    August 5 _____   August 8 _____

4. How many even-numbered days are in August? _____

5. How many Sundays are in August this year? _____

6. How many weekdays are there this year in August? (Weekdays are all the days from Monday to Friday.) _____

7. How many syllables are in the name *August*? _____

8. Circle all the calendar words below that have the same number of syllables.

April	May	June	July
Sunday	Saturday	Thursday	February
week	Friday	holiday	weekend
summer	spring	winter	autumn

Helper: _____

Due: _____

Set Sail!

Skill

Visual perception, noting details

The United States celebrates Columbus Day every October, to mark the anniversary of the discovery of America. But did you know that his long journey began more than two months earlier? In fact, Columbus and his crew set sail from Spain on August 3, 1492, with three ships. Here is one ship that may be like the one Columbus used. Complete the other two ships so that all three are the same. Have your family helper check your work.

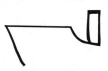

August 3

Anniversary of departure of Columbus

Due: _____

Helper: _____

August Riddle

The first Monday in August is the beginning of a special week. It is National __ __ __ __ __ Week! To find the five letters that belong in the blanks, solve each riddle below. Your family helper can assist you in finding each letter. The word bank will help you.

Skill
Word play

1. Find the letter that is in [sock] but not in [clock] . _____

2. Find the letter that is in [team] but not in [tea] . _____

3. Find the letter that is in [pie] but not in [pen] . _____

4. Find a letter that is in [log] but not in [goat] . _____

5. Find a letter that is in [bell] but not in [ball] . _____

Word Bank
goat
tea
ball
clock
log
pie
bell
team
sock
pen

**First Week
in August**

Can you and your family helper think of a riddle like the one above for one of these words: *cat, dog, sun, fish*?

Helper: _____

Due: _____

Smile!

The first Monday in August begins National Smile Week. A great way to be sure you have a nice smile is to take good care of your teeth. Unscramble each sentence to find a tip about caring for your teeth. Work with your family helper to write each sentence correctly.

1. your after Brush meals teeth

   _____

2. months dentist Visit six your every

   _____

3. floss Use brush you after

   _____

4. apples healthy foods Eat like carrots and

   _____

5. eat of sugary a lot Don't food

   _____

Due: _____

Helper: _____

Waffle Words

Skill

Spelling

On August 24, 1869, a man received the first patent for a waffle iron. In honor of this day, here are some "waffle" words for you and your family helper to find. Here's how.

- Start at any letter and move one space in any direction to another letter that is next to it.

- Don't go back to the same space in any one word, but use the letters over and over for different words.

As an example, look at the lines which connect the letters in *butter*. (You can also move diagonally.)

Now look for these words in the puzzle with your family helper. Circle the ones you find. You will not be able to spell all of them.

| maple | syrup | apples | batter | fruit |
| toaster | eat | snack | yummy | breakfast |

K	P	T	O	R
M	U	S	A	E
M	R	Y	T	T
Y	A	B	U	I
E	L	P	F	R

What is your favorite waffle topping? _____

August 24

Anniversary of patent of waffle iron

Helper: _____

Due: _____

Summer Sounds

Each of these summertime pictures names a word with the *SH* sound. If the *SH* sound comes at the beginning of the word, color the picture. If the *SH* sound comes at the end of the word, circle the picture.

Skill

Sh sound

Summer

With your family helper, list more *SH* words on the back.

Due: _____   Helper: _____

Summer Scenes

Which scenes below look like ones you could see in the summertime? Talk about your choices with your family helper. Then color only the summer scenes.

Skill

Recognizing seasons

Summer

Helper: _____

A Memorable Day at the Beach

Skill

Observation, memory

Fold this paper back on the dashed line so you can see only the top. Study the picture for one minute, trying to remember as many details as possible. Then have your family helper ask you the questions at the bottom of the page. Check your answers together in the picture.

Summer

1. How many people were in the water? _____

2. What else was in the water? _____

3. How many people were building the sand castle? _____

4. What shape was on the front of the sand pail? _____

5. What food was on the picnic table? _____

6. What time was the game going to be? _____

7. What was in the sky? _____

8. How many starfish were on the beach? _____

Due: _____   Helper: _____

TLC10119 Copyright © Teaching & Learning Company, Carthage, IL 62321-0010

Travel Tips

Several mistakes have been made on this summer travel brochure. Circle the ones you find.

Now design your own brochure for a place your family might like to visit. Try to get everything right!

**This sumer,
why not
come too sea**

THE

MAGICAL

SARFISH!

**Only in sunnytown,
U.S.a.**

**Open 9 a.m.-5 a.m.
7 days a week
(Closed Sunday)
Also swim at our beach!**

OPEN ALL WINTER

Summer

Helper: _____

Due: _____

Surf Search

Find these summertime words in the puzzle. Words can be spelled forwards, backwards, up, down or diagonally. Circle each word you find. Your family helper may want to find some, too!

Skill

Finding hidden words

bucket
shovel
sand
shells
sun
beach
water

shore
waves
water ski
swim
dive
picnic
float

sailing
surfing
starfish
seaweed
sunglasses
sand castles
life jacket

pool
lifeguard
swimsuit
towel
fun

Summer

L I F E J A C K E T F N
S I C I N C I P S U S U
T U F B E A C H N E W S
A B N E Q K E T L O A P
R U S G G L I T E G T O
F C U X L U S F W N E O
I K R S S A A B O I R L
S E F M C Z S R T L S E
H T I D I V E S D I K V
V W N T A O L F E A I O
S A G W A T E R G S J H
S H O R E D E E W A E S
S E V A W M I W S A N D

Helper: _____

Answer Key

Rhyming Riddles, page 12

1. fat cat, 2. free tree, 3. wet pet, 4. sweet beet, 5. right night,
6. tan can, 7. glad dad

Phone Math, page 16

1. 43 cents, 2. 35 cents, 3. 33 cents, 4. 44 cents, 5. 42 cents, 6. 32 cents,
7. 26 cents

Coded Message, page 17

Mr. Watson, come here. I want you.

Who Was St. Patrick? page 20

3, 6, 1, 5, 2, 7, 4

Speaking of Irish . . . , page 21

snow = sneachta, house = teach, spoon = spúnóg, children = napáistí, one = haon,
dog = madra, welcome = failte, hair = gruaig, mouse = luch, five = cuig,
water = uisce, fish = iasc, swan = eala

Map of Ireland, page 22

A. Londonderry, B. Belfast, C. Galway, D. Dublin, E. Limerick, F. Waterford,
G. Cork, H. Atlantic Ocean, I. St. George's Channel, J. Irish Sea

Growing Plans, page 25

Vania–tomatoes, Caleb–corn, Rowena–wheat, Phil–cattle, Dale–sheep

Coloring Egg, page 26

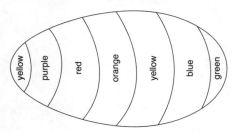

Baby Animals, page 28

1. calf, 2. pup, 3. kitten, 4. kid, 5. chick, 6. cub, 7. lamb, 8. fawn, 9. duckling,
10. foal

Bunnies and Eggs, page 29

Possible answers include:
1. funny, money, honey, runny, sunny
2. beaver, bat, badger, bull, bobcat, bear, etc.
3. scrambled, fried, over-easy, poached, hard-boiled, soft-boiled, deviled, omelet,
   etc.
4. east, eastern, easel, eager, each, etc.
5. shell, yolk, white
6. chickens, robins, geese, turkeys, ostriches, turtles, crocodiles, etc.

Fair for Four, page 30

1. doll; 2. apple; 3. Teri, Carrie, Shari; 4. lollipop, Shari; 5. Teri

Animal Antics, page 33

1. H, 2. D, 3. F, 4. A, 5. J, 6. I, 7. B, 8. E, 9. G, 10. C

Hidden Numbers, page 37

Where has the fa**t wo**rm g**one**? He was wriggling away from my re**el even** before I had the hook on it! I**f I've** lost him, I'll be sorry. Thi**s even**ing I came prepared wi**th ree**l, line and bait hoping to catch plenty of fish. It's not of**ten** that a worm of **our**s gets away!

Picture Pairs, page 39

Trash Cash, page 40

1. 26 cents, 2. 14 cents, 3. 24 cents, 4. 31 cents, 5. 28 cents, 6. 36 cents, 7. 50 cents, 8. 33 cents, 9. 34 cents, 10. 41 cents

Triangle Trouble, page 42

There are 10 triangles.

Boston Marathon, page 44

1. east, 2. south, 3. southwest, 4. Answers will vary.

Date Data, page 45

1897

May Flowers, page 46

1. A, C; 2. B; 3. E; 4. D

Criss-Crossed Sports, page 49

Across: 3. soccer, 4. football, 6. swimming, 7. basketball, 9. hockey, 10. volleyball
Down: 1. tennis, 2. baseball, 3. skiing, 5. bowling, 8. archery

Hoop Shoot, page 50

A. 13, B. 8, C. 13, D. 14, E. 11, F. 5, G. 10, H. 8, Team Total: 82

Family Tree, page 53

1. 5; 2. 2; 3. 0; 4. 2; 5. 2, Joe, Tom; 6. 3; 7. 2; 8. 3; 9. 2

In or On? page 54

1. in, 2. on, 3. in, 4. on, 5. on, 6. in or on, 7. in, 8. on, 9. in

A to Z Animals, page 55

Possible answers include: alligator, bear, cow, dog, eagle, fox, gerbil, horse, iguana, jackal, kangaroo, lion, mouse, newt, orangutan, penguin, quail, rabbit, seal, turtle, vulture, walrus, yak, zebra

Five Facts, page 58

1. 10, 2. 60, 3. 50, 4. 5, 5. 15, 6. 20, 7. 55, 8. 0, 9. 50, 10. 25

Sweet Treats, page 60

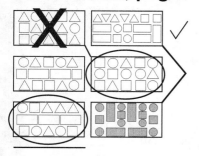

Ages and Stages, page 64

1. 1973 - 1951 = 22, 2. 1978 - 1951 = 27, 3. 1983 - 1951 = 32, 4. 1987 - 1951 = 36, 5. Answers will vary.

Memorial Mayhem, page 65

States, women, country, years, people, May, Monday

visit, flowers, parades, trucks, park, picnics, race, Memorial

Spot the Butterflies, page 66

Bargain Hunting, page 69

Ron: 40 cents–stamps, Kim: 36 cents–car, Jed: 29 cents–baseball card, Bruce: 52 cents–wallet, Darnell: 48 cents–book

Plan a Plot, page 70

Answers may vary. Here is one possibility.

Score It, page 71

The final score was Badgers 6, Coyotes 7; Coyotes won.

Fatherly Facts, page 77

1. true, 2. true, 3. false, 4. true, 5. false, 6. false, 7. false, 8. true

Sit Fit, page 79

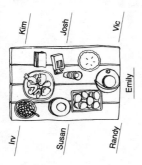

The Fourth Challenge, page 81

Possible answers include:

Three-Letter Words: for, rot, hot, lot, hut, fur, fry, joy, our, you, off

Four-Letter Words: hoof, hoot, foot, loft, four, fort, tour, hour, fury, jury, your, turf

Longer Words: froth, forth, forty, flour, truly

August Riddle, page 85

1. S, 2. M, 3. I, 4. L, 5. E, National Smile Week

Smile! page 86

1. Brush your teeth after meals.
2. Visit your dentist every six months.
3. Use floss after you brush.
4. Eat healthy foods like carrots and apples.
5. Don't eat a lot of sugary food.

Waffle Words, page 87

You should be able to find these words: *maple, syrup, fruit, toaster, eat, yummy.*

A Memorable Day at the Beach, page 90

1. three; 2. sailboat; 3. one; 4. heart; 5. watermelon; 6. 3:00 p.m.; 7. sun, birds;
8. five

Surf Search, page 92

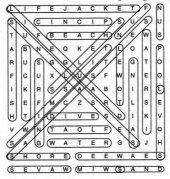